I0824287

ATHENEUM BOOKS FOR YOUNG READERS
An imprint of Simon & Schuster Children's Publishing Division
1230 Avenue of the Americas, New York, New York 10020

Book design by Greg Stadnyk

The text for this book was set in Gelica.
The illustrations for this book were rendered digitally.
Manufactured in China
1125 SCP
First Edition
2 4 6 8 10 9 7 5 3 1
CIP data for this book is available from the Library of Congress.
ISBN 9781665946704
ISBN 9781665946711 (ebook)

For all the future organizers and fighters for justice —A. Q. P.

For my parents and Scout: Thank you for inspiring my voice —S. S.

Author Acknowledgments

Special thanks to Jessica's nephew Juan Govea; Georgetown University professor Dr. Mireya Loza; and Mary J. Wallace, audiovisual archivist at Walter P. Reuther Library, for the helpful information and resources they provided during my research on Jessica.

FROM THE FIELDS TO THE FIGHT

How Jessica Govea Thorbourne Organized for Justice

Written by Angela Quezada Padron
Illustrated by Sol Salinas

atheneum

Atheneum Books for Young Readers
New York Amsterdam/Antwerp London Toronto Sydney/Melbourne New Delhi

Every summer morning

before the California sun rose, Jessica and her family went to the fields to pick crops. Her parents were Mexican American and had been working in the fields for years. But they were paid just a few dollars a day. Now they needed Jessica's help to earn more. Like other families hoping for work, they would do their jobs with dignity.

Hundreds of migrants standing in line.
One tired little girl waiting to lend a hand.

Jessica followed in her parents' footsteps. Her tiny hands plucked cotton, dragged heavy sacks, and clipped grapes from the vines. She crawled on the ground, scooping up plums as they rained down from trees and dodging stinging wasps.

One resilient girl working beside
other children doing what was needed.

Year after year, Jessica continued to pick crops. But life in the fields wasn't easy.

The days were long and hot. Workers got little pay. Their bellies grumbled from hunger, and their bodies ached. There was no bathroom nearby. And chemical pesticides meant to kill plant-eating bugs seeped into everyone's hair, clothes, and skin—including Jessica's.

As Jessica grew up, she saw her community struggling. Classmates at school were punished for not speaking English. Some had to leave school to work in the fields. Migrant families couldn't find decent homes or good doctors to care for them. Many were treated poorly just because they were Latino.

One concerned community, longing for change,
unsure how to fight for equal rights . . .

Until one day . . .

. . . a visitor came to town. His name was Cesar Chavez.

Cesar used to be a child worker in the fields, just like Jessica. He understood the struggles of poor farmworkers. He wanted to empower communities to seek fairness and justice.

But he was just one man.
He needed people to join the cause.

Jessica's parents signed up. Jessica was eager to get involved too.

But she was just one child. What could she do?

She could learn.

Jessica went door-to-door with her father. They listened to neighbors' hardships and passed out flyers. As her father convinced others to join Cesar, Jessica paid close attention.

One observant girl, focused and curious, learning how to organize a movement.

2

As she got older, Jessica became a leader. She spoke in front of crowds, led other kids to petition for a neighborhood park, and practiced defending her ideas.

Some people refused to speak to her. But Jessica didn't give up. She listened and persisted, just like her father had shown her.

One determined girl
making a difference,
wanting to do even more.

Meanwhile, Cesar and his friend Dolores Huerta met with other activists. Many of them were Filipino farmworkers who had built their own union years before.

They joined together to create an even bigger labor union to protect farmworkers and fight for their rights.

The union workers went on strike against grape growers in Delano, California. They refused to pick any more grapes for the growers to sell unless they got higher pay. If the growers didn't listen, the grapes would rot in the fields. The growers would lose money.

One tiny fruit, the center of the fight, giving the union hope.

But instead of listening, the growers hired other people to pick the grapes. Many farmworkers lost their jobs and homes. They were afraid of not being able to care for their families.

The union had to keep trying. But they needed more people to protest.

Cesar and Dolores went to different neighborhoods, encouraging more families to join the cause. Sometimes everyone met at Jessica's house.

Jessica felt inspired. She wanted to work for the union.

Her father said no. He wanted her to finish her college education.

But Jessica stood her ground. College would have to wait. Like father, like daughter; she knew this was what she was meant to do.

So did he.

One proud father.
One steadfast daughter
ready to organize for
justice.

Jessica got to work. She traveled to different places in California, encouraging workers to stop picking grapes until the growers treated them better. She energized large crowds by singing and reciting poetry. She went to the fields and protested.

But the growers still weren't listening. Jessica and the union had to do more.

The union started a boycott. They asked customers not to buy products made by the growers until those companies treated workers better.

A few customers, then a few more, stopped buying those products. Soon many people stopped. The boycott made one company lose too much money, so they agreed to work with the union.

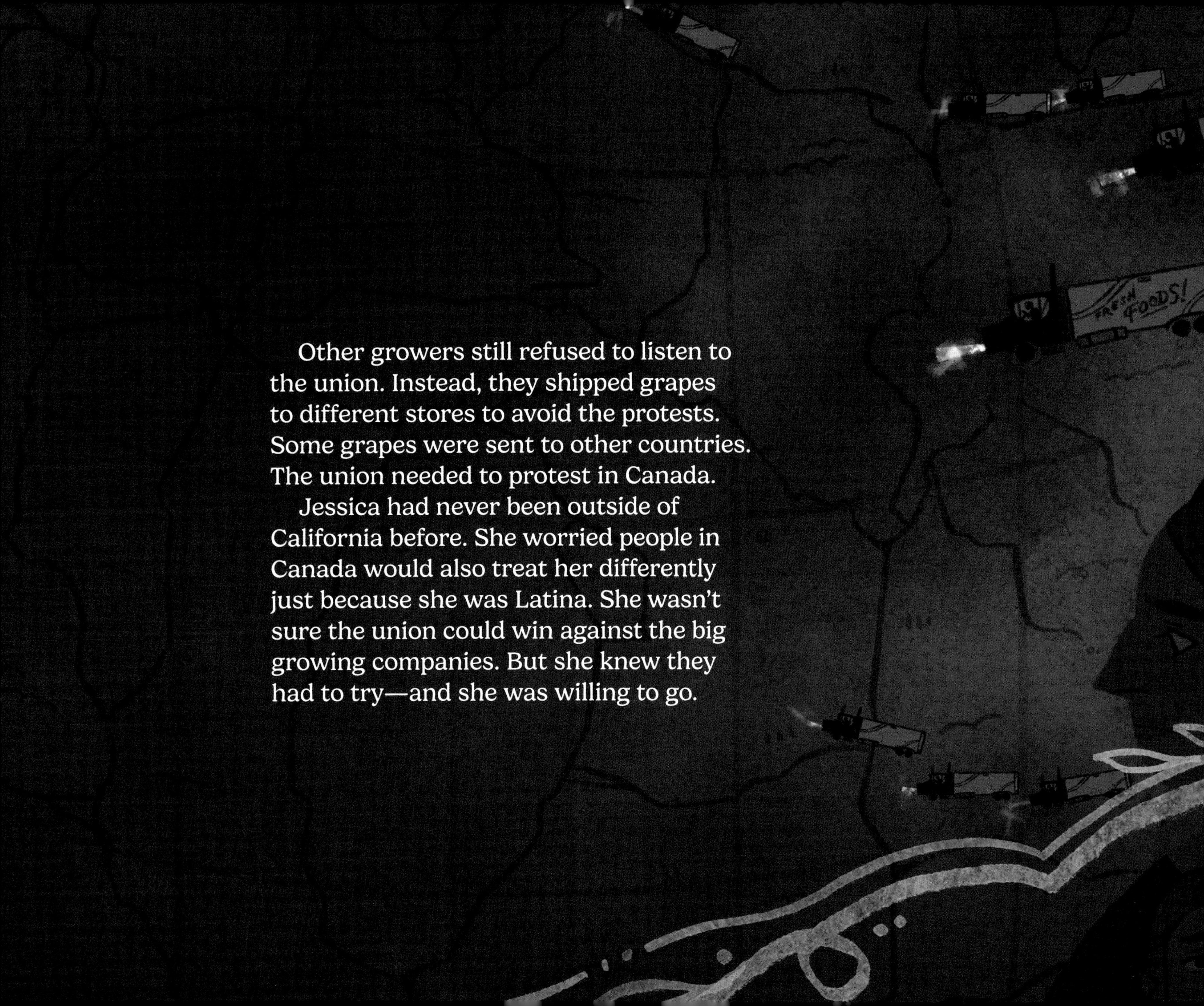

Other growers still refused to listen to the union. Instead, they shipped grapes to different stores to avoid the protests. Some grapes were sent to other countries. The union needed to protest in Canada.

Jessica had never been outside of California before. She worried people in Canada would also treat her differently just because she was Latina. She wasn't sure the union could win against the big growing companies. But she knew they had to try—and she was willing to go.

One brave woman putting her fears
aside to do what was needed for justice.

Jessica found people in Canada who let her stay in their homes, but sometimes she had to sleep on the floor. Sometimes she barely had enough food to eat.

She missed her family. She was so far away from home.

One lonely fighter crying herself to sleep, almost ready to give up.

But Jessica remembered all the hardships Latinos in her community faced. She thought about her time working in the fields and how unfairly she and other farmworkers had been treated.

She had to keep fighting for justice, even if she stood up alone.

But she wasn't alone. She found people willing to join her.

Day after day, Jessica and her team protested outside grocery stores, passed out flyers, asked for donations, and encouraged customers not to buy California grapes. Every person who joined gave them a bigger chance to make a difference.

The boycott went on for weeks that turned into months.

Jessica was exhausted, but she wouldn't stop until the union won.

Jessica told Canadians about the farmworkers' stories. Other union workers in Canada came to support the protests. Jessica and her team convinced more and more people to join the boycott.

One customer stopped buying grapes, and soon many people in Canada followed.

Sales of grapes dropped everywhere. The growers lost money as the movement spread.

So the growers finally listened.

After years of protesting, boycotting, voting, striking, and uniting, workers got higher pay, better working conditions, and medical care. The union had succeeded!

And so had Jessica.

One courageous woman doing her part for justice.

Throughout her life, Jessica stood up for fairness and empowered people to demand change.

Jessica showed that making a difference . . .

. . . can start with just one child.

ABOUT JESSICA

Jessica Govea Thorbourne was born in 1947 in Porterville, California. At age four, she started picking crops with her parents.

At the time, there were child labor laws to protect children. However, the laws didn't apply to children working in agriculture. Because adult farmworkers, who were mostly Latino and Asian, were paid very little—sometimes less than one dollar per hour—many parents brought their children along to work.

Jessica and the other children were forced to labor in dangerous conditions to help their families earn more money. Many workers became sick from the chemicals in pesticides. Others suffered from hunger or heat exhaustion. Even if they got hurt on the job, they had to keep working.

When Jessica was twelve years old, she began to organize for change. Her best friend, Virginia, was struck by a car on her way home from the park, which was three miles away. Jessica didn't want that to happen to anyone else. She rallied her friends, and they went door-to-door with a petition for a new park closer to their homes.

From there, Jessica continued to build organizing skills. She taught herself to type so she could create leaflets encouraging her neighbors to vote or attend organizing meetings. She helped people register to vote; campaigned for government officials like Governor Jerry Brown in California and Senator Robert Kennedy, who wanted to pass laws to protect workers; and spoke out against the dangers of pesticides.

For sixteen years, Jessica joined Cesar Chavez and Dolores Huerta in their fight to help farmworkers receive fair wages and treatment. She wanted to end discrimination against Latinos. When she got older, Jessica continued to fight for justice by teaching community groups, laborers, and college students how to organize.

Sadly, there was one battle she struggled to win. In 2005, Jessica died from cancer. She believed her illness was caused by years of exposure to pesticides in the fields.

Jessica inspired many people to work together for equality. She showed that a person of any age can impact the lives of others.

Important Words to Know

Child labor laws are meant to protect the health, safety, and educational opportunities of children. Today these laws still do not completely protect children in agriculture. In some states, children as young as twelve years old can work in fields or on farms. In other states where laws are not well enforced, children younger than twelve are often working.

Pesticides are chemicals used to kill insects that eat and destroy crops. Certain chemicals from pesticides have been known to cause illness in animals and humans, including cancer.

People **protest** when they object to something. Protests can be done in many ways, such as marches, rallies, and petitions. Under the US Constitution, people have the right to assemble and protest in peaceful ways.

Strikes and **boycotts** are types of protests. In a **strike**, workers refuse to go back to their jobs until their bosses or managers agree to listen to their concerns. When people **boycott**, they refuse to buy, resell, or use a product or service, in order to encourage a change in policies.

A **union** is a group of workers who come together to make sure they are treated fairly at their jobs. They join together to advocate for better pay, benefits, and safe working conditions.

How Can You Organize?

- Decide on a cause. What do you want to change in your own community, across the country, or around the world?
- Research the issue. Write down facts and data.
- Find family members, friends, and classmates who might be interested in helping. Work together to brainstorm things you could do to bring about change. These could include:
    - Holding fundraisers
    - Passing out flyers or hanging posters around the neighborhood
    - Creating a blog to spread the word
    - Arranging a community event to share information
    - Creating T-shirts with a message
    - Contacting your local news stations
- Look for organizations that are involved in this issue. See if they can give you information or helpful hints. Maybe you can join forces to bring about change!

Timeline of the United Farmworkers (UFW) Labor Union

1959 The Agricultural Workers Organizing Committee (AWOC) is founded by mostly Filipino farmworkers who had fought against unfair labor practices for farmworkers in the 1930s and 1940s.

March 1962 Cesar Chavez leaves the Community Service Organization (CSO), whose founder, Fred Ross, fought for all Latinos' civil rights and trained Cesar to organize. Cesar wants to focus on organizing for farmworkers.

September 1962 Cesar Chavez and Dolores Huerta hold the first convention of the National Farmworkers Association (NFWA) in California.

September 1965 The NFWA joins the AWOC in a strike against grape growers in Delano, California.

December 1965 The NFWA calls for its first boycott of processed grapes grown by Schenley Industries, the second largest grower in Delano.

1966 Jessica Govea joins the NFWA as an organizer at the age of nineteen.

April 1966 Schenley Industries becomes the first major grape grower to recognize the farmworkers' unions. It agrees to give workers better working conditions and wages.

August 1966 The AWOC and the NFWA officially join forces to become the United Farmworkers Organizing Committee (UFWOC), which is later known simply as the United Farmworkers (UFW). They continue to strike and boycott different grape growers.

January 1968 The UFW calls for a boycott of California table grapes across the US.

July 1968 Jessica Govea heads to Canada with other UFW members to lead grape boycotts there.

July 1970 Many grape growers in California sign contracts with the UFW. Farmworkers get higher wages and healthcare benefits. They also are protected from exposure to pesticides.